ENGLISH PRACTICE AND PROGRESS

VOCABULARY ACTIVITIES
(PRE-INTERMEDIATE – INTERMEDIATE)

JULIE WOODWARD

SCHOLASTIC

MARY GLASGOW MAGAZINES

Contents

Classroom Equipment

Look at the pictures below. Under each picture are two letters. By matching the words in the list below with the pictures you can spell out the mystery proverb.

For example: blackboard   +   rubbish bin

Wo   +   rd   =   word

th   ee   tc   he   ly

ar   rd   bi

ca   rm   he   wo   st

The proverb

poster + desk + computer + globe + scissors + rubbish bin

....

+ notebook + glue + stapler + chalk + rubber + blackboard + pencil

....

Clue: *There are six words in the proverb.*

What does the proverb mean?

1   The first person to arrive will have the best opportunities. ☐
or
2   The first person to arrive will have plenty to eat. ☐

Who's Who?

1. Read the information below and find out who is who in the classroom. Write the pupils' names on their desks. Rearrange the circled letters to find out what subject they are studying.

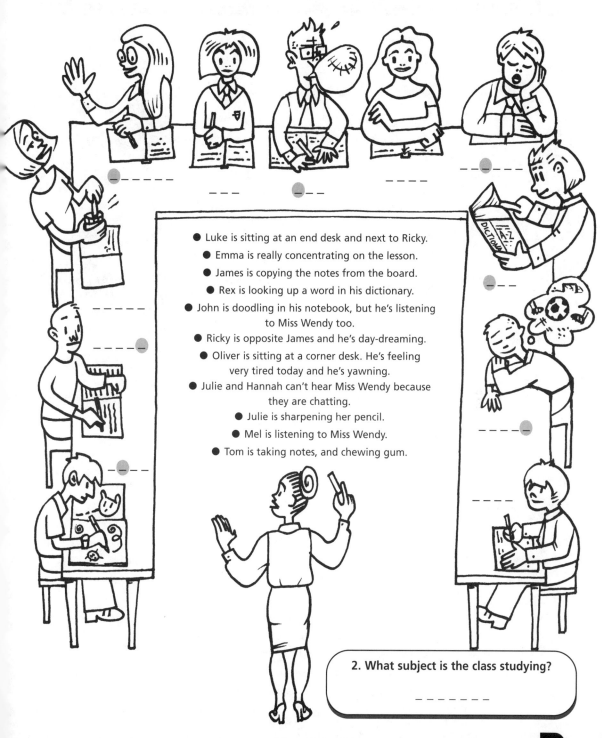

- Luke is sitting at an end desk and next to Ricky.
- Emma is really concentrating on the lesson.
- James is copying the notes from the board.
- Rex is looking up a word in his dictionary.
- John is doodling in his notebook, but he's listening to Miss Wendy too.
- Ricky is opposite James and he's day-dreaming.
- Oliver is sitting at a corner desk. He's feeling very tired today and he's yawning.
- Julie and Hannah can't hear Miss Wendy because they are chatting.
- Julie is sharpening her pencil.
- Mel is listening to Miss Wendy.
- Tom is taking notes, and chewing gum.

2. What subject is the class studying?

_ _ _ _ _ _ _

School Diary

Here are some of the things Janice and Jamie have recently done at school, and also some of the things they are going to do in the next month.

1. First, match the expressions below in the box with the correct pictures.

a. exams	b. disco	c. detention	d. sports day	e. school outing	f. uniform-free day

g. biology field trip
h. after-school study class
i. rehearsals for school play
j. police visit

**2. Today it's the 3rd of April.
Write the dates for these events.**

1. Jamie had a history exam the day before yesterday. .... *April 1st*
2. Next Monday Janice is going on a biology field trip. ....
3. Exactly a month ago Janice had a detention after school because she had been late. ....
4. The day after tomorrow is the annual sports day. ....
5. In a fortnight's time the rehearsals are going to start for the school play. ....
6. This time next month Janice and Jamie will be in London, on the school outing. ....
7. This time next week nobody will be wearing their school uniforms ....
8. Jamie studied maths after school last Thursday. ....
9. There is a visit from the police tomorrow morning to talk about road safety. ....
10. The end-of-term disco is on the last Friday in May. ....

A Tour of England

Look at Olivier's holiday photos from his trip to England. Write the correct words in the text. The numbers correspond to the numbers in the photo.

Useful vocabulary

hotel
coach
ferry
local specialities
bikes
tour guide
nightlife
scenery
sea view
sightseeing
monuments

Last month our class spent a week touring England. We took the (1)...............

and the crossing wasn't too rough. For the first few nights we stayed in a little (2)

.... with a nice (3)................ . We travelled around the country in a (4)

.................., and we had a really funny (5).............. called Rex. My favourite day

was when we rented (6) .... and cycled through the countryside in North

Devon. The (7) .... was breathtaking. We visited London, of course,

where we saw lots of (8) .... and did lots of (9) .... - and we

saw the Thames too. We tried some (10) .... every day – my favourite

was the fish and chips we had during our excursion to Windsor. On our last night

Rex organised a big party with a group of secondary school students so we could

enjoy some English (11) ....

On Holiday

Across

2.   A 'house on wheels' pulled by your car

3.   What you do on arrival at the airport

4.   A holday spent at sea aboard a luxury ship

5.   A special 'bus' used for tourism

7.   When the plane leaves the ground

9.   The person who flies the plane

10.   You need this if you travel abroad

12.   In the plane you can have window seat or an .... seat

13.   A popular holiday water sport

17.   If your flight doesn't leave on time, it is ....

18.   You do this when you visit museums and monuments

21.   During their holidays some people like to do nothing except ....

25.   Your accommodation when you go camping

26.   The person who shows you around and informs you about a place

27.   Holiday for a couple who have just got married

28.   The place to go to build sandcastles and sunbathe

29.   Luxurious accommodation

Down

1.   Magazine offering different holidays

6.   When there are just too many tourists it is ....

8.   A person from a different country from yours

9.   Before going away you must do this

11.   When you go walking on a .... holiday you are doing this

14.   The place where you pitch your tent

15.   A large ship which transports holiday makers and their cars

16.   People like to do this during their winter holidays in the snow

19.   Shop which sells holidays

20.   You should put this on your skin if you don't want the sun to burn you

22.   To reserve your holiday

23.   The place where young people can stay cheaply

24.   Official border control when you travel to another country

The Return Home

1. Four people have just got back from their holidays abroad. Mr and Mrs Brown, James and Lucy are unpacking their luggage. Look at the pictures of each and say five things about what each person did on their holiday, using the verbs in the box. For example: James visited Italy.

film	take photos
dive	speak a foreign language
listen to music	sunbathe
read	hike
go sightseeing	
paint	go cycling
swim	visit
go on a guided tour	relax
camp	pitch a tent
	send postcards

2. Are these sentences true (T) or false (F)?

1 Mr and Mrs Brown slept in a cabin. ☐

2 Lucy can't swim. ☐

3 James stayed in a hotel. ☐

4 Mr and Mrs Brown went to Africa. ☐

5 Mr and Mrs Smith travelled by plane. ☐

6 Lucy enjoys sport. ☐

7 James did plenty of walking. ☐

8 All of them expected sunny weather. ☐

Enjoying the Arts

1. All these people have been enjoying something arty – going to the theatre, visiting a museum, watching a film etc. But the dialogues are all mixed up. Can you put the dialogues with the correct speakers?

---

2. What have these people just done?

Join the sentences and match them with the correct pictures above.

They've just...

☐ read	a play	on the radio.
☐ visited	a film	in a magazine.
☐ seen	an exhibition	on TV.
☐ listened to	an article	at the theatre.
☐ watched	the news	at an art gallery.
☐ seen	a programme	at the cinema.

3. Look for the eleven letters on the people's clothes. Arrange the letters to find out the name of one of England's most famous playwrights.

– – – – – – – – – – –

Know your music

Find the answers to these musical definitions hidden in the hexagons and then test your knowledge in the music quiz below.

A live musical performance is a

_____ .

9

The words to a song are called

_____ .

10

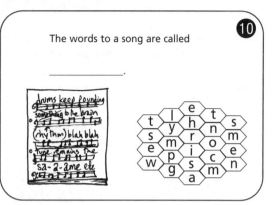

MUSIC QUIZ

1. Which famous British pop group was made up of John Lennon, Paul McCartney, George Harrison and Ringo Starr? . . . .

2. Who composed *The Four Seasons*: Vivaldi or Beethoven? . . . .

3. Did Louis Armstrong play the trumpet or the piano? . . . .

4. Liam Gallagher is the lead singer for which band? REM or Oasis? . . . .

5. Celine Dion sang on the soundtrack for which Oscar-winning film? . . . .

6. He's a singer and an actor famous for *Men in Black*. Is his name Michael Jackson or Will Smith?

. . . .

7. What nationality is the opera singer Luciano Pavarotti? . . . .

8. Is the national anthem for Great Britain *God Save Everybody* or *God Save the Queen*?

. . . .

9. Was Bob Marley a folk singer or a reggae singer? . . . .

10. At Christmas people sing special songs called Christmas carols. True or false? . . . .

At the Bookshop

1. The people in the bookshop need some help in deciding what to buy. First, unscramble the letters to find the title of each section.

2. Now read what the people are saying and suggest what books for them to buy.

For example: Tom should buy ___Elvis, the Boy___

Geoff should buy _ _ _ _ _ _ _ _ _ _ _ _ _ _ _ _ _

James should buy _ _ _ _ _ _ _ _ _ _ _ _ _ _ _ _ _

Danny should buy _ _ _ _ _ _ _ _ _ _ _ _ _ _ _ _

Sally should buy _ _ _ _ _ _ _ _ _ _ _ _ _ _ _ _ _ _ _

Sarah should buy _ _ _ _ _ _ _ _ _ _ _ _ _ _ _ _ _ _

Julia should buy _ _ _ _ _ _ _ _ _ _ _ _ _ _ _ _ _ _

Kate should buy _ _ _ _ _ _ _ _ _ _ _ _ _ _ _ _ _

Film Buff

1. Are you a film buff/cinema addict? Have you seen these films?

E.T. **JAWS** The Titanic Star Wars *Psycho* **GLADIATOR**

Saving Private Ryan THE TERMINATOR INDIANA JONES Romeo & Juliet

> I saw a terrific film at the weekend.
>
> What was it?

Calvin Jane Bryn Lucy

> *Titanic*, it's an Oscar-winning film.
>
> Oh, yes, it's got great special effects; very sad though. I love romantic films.

> Although I really enjoyed *Titanic*, my favourite types of films are horror and thrillers.
>
> I prefer science fiction films.
>
> I love war films. I like learning about history.

2. Look at the film genres below. Match each genre and its definition.

Horror	A love story. The main characters usually fall in love with each other but their relationships usually have some difficulties.
Science Fiction	The story portrays a period in the past with costumes and scenery of that time.
Action	Monsters, ugly creatures and blood. Lots of special effects to frighten you.
Historical	Fast and exciting. Very often the main character is a superhero trying to save the world.
Romantic	The story is set in the future and often has fantastic gadgets to make you dream.
War	A film with lots of suspense, psychological games and mystery.
Thriller	Plenty of action in the Wild West. The lives of cowboys, sheriffs and sometimes Native Americans.
Comedy	Funny situations and witty dialogues to make you laugh.
Western	Battles and fighting are the main features of this type of film. Very often it portrays a real battle in the past.

3. The four teenagers have each decided to rent a video for the evening. Which person takes the films below?

Romeo & Juliet _

Psycho _

Saving Private Ryan _

Star Wars _

Our Free Time

It's Friday night – no school for two days! Everyone is preparing their bags for Saturday morning when they will do their favourite free time activity. Look at the pictures and say what they are going to do. Use the clues under the pictures to help you.

go

He's going to go fishing.

go

go

go

do some

He's going to do some photography.

Use the verbs at the sides of the pictures and choose the correct unscrambled words to make going to sentences.

1. eth tuirag 2. cidnang 3. nisten 4. gidrin
5. ggigonj 6. mingwism 7. shingif 8. deovi magse
9. lerlor tingkas 10. intaping 11. sesch 12. ingvid
13. phyragothop 14. wingirdbacht

do some

go

He's going to go diving.

go

go

go

play

She's going to play tennis.

play

play

play

On the Road

Match the words and their definitions. Then use the corresponding directions to trace the route on the map. If you choose the correct definitions, you will arrive at the right finishing point. However, if you make a mistake, you will get lost!

1. traffic jam
a. Lots of cars not moving in the street.
b. Food that you eat in your car on long journeys.

2. rush hour
a. A quiet time to drive.
b. The time when the roads are very busy.

3. motorway
a. A special road for motorbikes.
b. A large road for fast travel between cities.

4. break down
a. The car has a mechanical problem and stops.
b. When the driver is so stressed he/she can't drive.

a. Move forward to the first junction.
b. Move forward to the second junction on the left.

a. Turn left, go forward to the second junction.
b. Turn left, go forward to the next junction.

a. Turn left, go straight on, stop at the junction.
b. Turn right and go straight on to the next junction.

a. Turn left, stop at the next junction.
b. Turn left, stop at the next junction.

5. pavement
a. A place for cars to park.
b. The side of the road where people walk.

6. brake
a. A pedal used to stop the car.
b. To stop driving and have a rest on long journeys.

7. overtake
a. When one car goes past the car in front.
b. When a car crashes into the car in front.

8. fill up
a. When the streets are full of people and the cars can't pass.
b. To put petrol in the car.

a. Go straight on, stop at the second junction.
b. Turn left, stop at the next junction.

a. Turn right, stop at the roundabout.
b. Turn left, go on to the next junction.

a. Take the third exit on the left.
b. Turn left and stop at The first junction.

a. Turn right, then stop.
b. Go straight on and stop at the end of the road.

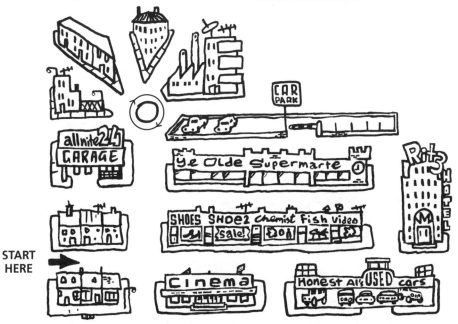

START HERE

In Town

1. If you look around town, you will see lots of different notices. Match the notices below to the numbered spaces in the town. We have done the first one for you.

a) No smoking ..6..   b) Quiet please! ......   c) Queue this side ......

d) We accept all major credit cards ......   e) £100 fine for dropping litter ......

f) Keep off the grass ......   g) No vacancies ......   h) Pay and display ......

i) Sale ......   j) Lunch now being served ......   k) No parking ......

CLOTHES

GReen GROCER

B+B

11

1

10% OFF

Library

Post Office

NEWSAGENT

BUTCHER

7

Chemist **BANK** BAKERY

TAXI

4

8

5

MCMAGS

TOWN

TAXI

6

CAR PARK

CAFE SOUVENIRS

2

10

3

STOP

9

2. Maggie has been into town this morning. Look at the contents of her bag. Where has she been?

Printer's Mix-Up

Eleven shops have placed an advertisement in the newspaper. Unfortunately, the printer has mixed up all the texts. Can you put the right advertisements with the right shops in the pictures?

Daily News Advertisements

S & J's Sandwich Bar

1. This week's special: finest British beef … go on, treat yourself!

Lorna's Ladies' Fashions

2. Freshly baked bread every day.

HAMMER HARDWARE STORE

3. Strawberries, raspberries, peaches, melons … summer's here at last! Get here fast!

Mr Watts Electrical Market

4. This week only! A free bottle of shampoo for every cut and blow dry.

Get Set Hairdresser's

5. Feeling tired? Come and try our special range of vitamins. Give your life a boost.

High Street Chemist's

6. 10% discount on children's sandals.

High Heels shoe shop

7. Magazines for everyone! From Art History to Zoology Monthly. We stock it!

Newsagent's

8. Delicious filled French bread or sliced bread. 30 fillings to choose from.

PORK CHOP – the butcher's shop

9. Buy a TV from us and get a second one free! Don't believe us? Come and see!

Rising Dough Baker's

10. Everything a woman could want to wear – and more…

Corner Greengrocer's

11. D.I.Y? Need help in your home? We've got the tools, if you've got the muscles!

Going Shopping

You are staying with your aunt and you offer to do the shopping for her. She gives you the shopping list below and a map of her village.

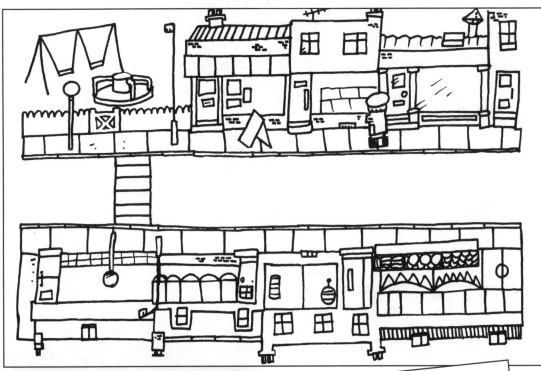

1. Which shops do you need to go to? Connect the items with the correct shop.

Items of shopping

bread rolls
butter
lettuce
pears
4 slices of ham
toothpaste
lottery ticket (numbers: 3 4 6 13 10 33)
rice
tin of mushroom soup

Shops

greengrocer's	butcher's	newsagent's
baker's	grocer's	chemist's

2. Use the clues to help you find the shops on the map.

- The butcher's is opposite the play area.
- The grocer's and the greengrocer's are at the end of the street.
- The café is between the greengrocer's and the chemist's.
- The newsagent's is next to the play area and opposite the chemist's.
- The baker's is opposite the café and next to the grocer's.

Summer Job

Richard has got a job at a local supermarket during his summer holidays. It's his first day at work today and his job is to stock the shelves. Look at all the products and put them in the correct place in the supermarket.

STOCKROOM

Dairy Products Delicatessen Fresh Meat Fresh Fish

Frozen Foods Poultry Beverages Groceries

Tinned Food Condiments Cleaning Products Toiletries Soft Drinks

Baby Products

Fresh Fruit and Vegetables Ready-made Meals

salt
ketchup
yoghurts
olive oil
salami
fresh olives
washing-up liquid
ice cream
shampoo
chops
Coca Cola
mackerel
rice
potatoes
Chinese meal for two

coffee
tinned tomatoes
cheese
pepper
milk
ham
frozen peas
nappies
chicken
toothpaste
sausages
apples
bananas
pasta
lasagne
tea

Household Gadgets

Look at the two pictures. They show the same house - and the changes after 50 years.
In 2002 there are lots of machines and gadgets to make life easier in the home.
Unscramble the letters to name the modern machines. Can you find them
in the 2002 house?

1. daroi mlaar cclko
2. obliem hpneo
3. teeiclcr hburttoosseh
4. rihearrdy
5. leevtoinsi & dovie
6. phteelnoe & xaf chmanei
7. mpcoteru & ntrepir
8. ttresoa
9. vcimeawro
10. hhresawisd
11. ignhsaw niehcma
12. fdgier-zfeeerr

In the Garden

Label the things in the garden by matching the halves of words below.

For example: Number 13   f o u n + t a i n = fountain

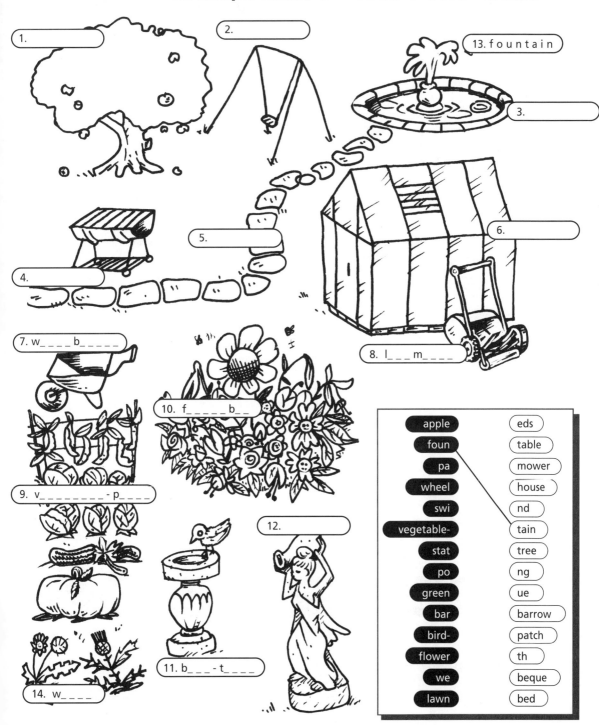

1.

2.

13. f o u n t a i n

3.

5.

4.

6.

7. w _ _ _ _ b _ _ _ _ _

8. l _ _ m _ _ _ _

10. f _ _ _ _ _ b _ _

9. v _ _ _ _ _ _ _ _ - p _ _ _ _

12.

11. b _ _ _ - t _ _ _ _

14. w _ _ _ _

apple	eds
foun	table
pa	mower
wheel	house
swi	nd
vegetable-	tain
stat	tree
po	ng
green	ue
bar	barrow
bird-	patch
flower	th
we	beque
lawn	bed

23

In the Right Place

1. Look at the pictures of the containers and different contents. Read the descriptions and match the content with the container.

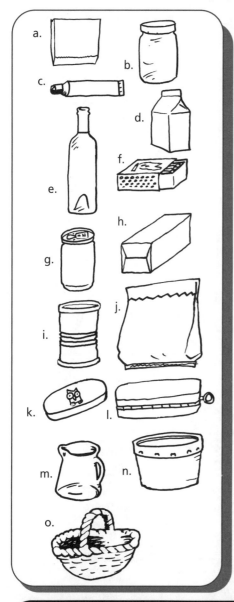

1. This case is made of plastic or leather. You keep spectacles (glasses) in it.

2. This bottle is made of glass. You buy wine in it.

3. This tube is made of plastic. You buy toothpaste in it.

4. A basket is made of plastic or cane and you put your shopping in it.

5. This tin is made of metal; you buy vegetables or fruit in it.

6. It's made of plastic and you can keep pens and pencils in it.

7. This little box is made of cardboard. You buy matches in it.

8. This carton is made of card for you to keep milk in.

9. This small container is made of glass. You buy jam and honey in it.

10. It's made of card or paper and it keeps biscuits or crisps fresh.

11. A glass jug is useful for serving water when you have a meal.

12. A tub is a round or rectangular container made of plastic to store margarine or ice cream.

13. This is a sack. You buy large quantities of potatoes in it.

14. This is made of paper or plastic and you put sweets in it.

15. This can is made of tin and it is for fizzy drinks.

2. How do we talk about containers for these things? Are the following right or wrong? If wrong, write the correction.

1. A jug of milk

2. A bottle of ice cream

3. A jar of coffee

4. A tin of peas

5. A case of carrots

6. A tube of beer

7. A can of lemonade

8. A box of chocolates

9. A tub of shampoo

Answers

Page 4
Classroom Equipment
The proverb is: *The early bird catches the worm.*

Page 5
Who's Who
The pupils from left to right, clockwise from bottom left-hand corner: John, James, Julie, Hannah, Mel, Tom, Emma, Oliver, Rex, Ricky, Luke
The subject being taught is history.

Page 6
School Diary
1) 1a 2e 3b 4g 5j 6h 7d 8i 9c 10f
2) 1 April 1st 2 April 8th 3 March 6th 4 April 5th 5 April 17th 6 May 1st 7 April 10th 8 March 28th 9 April 4th 10 May 31st

Page 7
A Tour of England
1 ferry 2 hotel 3 sea-view 4 coach 5 tour guide 6 bikes 7 scenery 8 monuments 9 sightseeing 10 local specialities 11 music

Pages 8 and 9
On Holiday
Across: 2 caravan 3 check-in 4 cruise 5 coach 7 take-off 9 pilot 10 passport 12 aisle 13 diving 17 delayed 18 sightseeing 21 relax 25 tent 26 tour-guide 27 honeymoon 28 beach 29 five-star-hotel
Down: 1 brochure 6 crowded 8 foreigner 11 hiking 14 campsite 15 ferry 16 ski 19 travel agent's 20 suncream 22 book 23 youth hostel 24 customs

Page 10
The Return Home
1) *Suggested answers:*
Mr and Mrs Brown went sightseeing in Egypt; filmed their cruise; read novels; relaxed; visited the Pyramids; stayed on a cruise ship
Lucy stayed in a hotel in Greece; went diving; swam; took photos; sunbathed; went sightseeing; saw the Acropolis; relaxed; listened to music
James camped in Italy; pitched a tent; hiked; spoke Italian; went sightseeing; sunbathed; relaxed
2) 1T 2F 3F 4T 5F 6T 7T 8T

Page 11
Enjoying the arts
1) Dialogue 1 with picture 3;
Dialogue 2 with picture 6
Dialogue 3 with picture 2;
Dialogue 4 with picture 5
Dialogue 5 with picture 1;
Dialogue 6 with picture 4

2) They've just
5 read an article in a magazine.
2 visited an exhibition at an art gallery.
1 seen a film at a cinema.
3 listened to the news on the radio.
4 watched a programme on TV.
6 seen a play at the theatre.

3) The eleven letters spell out *Shakespeare.*

Pages 12 and 13
Know Your Music
Hexagons: 1 guitarist 2 soundtrack 3 opera 4 vocalist 5 ballad 6 composer 7 duet 8 rap 9 concert 10 lyrics
Quiz: 1 The Beatles 2 Vivaldi 3 the trumpet 4 Oasis 5 *Titanic* 6 Will Smith 7 Italian 8 *God Save the Queen* 9 reggae 10 True

Page 14
At the Bookshop
1) science fiction, history, biography, drama, sport, horror, romance, poetry, crime
2) *Suggested answers:*
Tom – *Elvis, the Boy*
James – *The Second World War*
Sally – *Crimebuster*
Julia – *Flowers for Amy*
Geoff – *Blood in the Castle*
Danny – *Football's Greatest Goals*
Sarah – *Death of a Shop Assistant*
Kate – *Poems about Animals*

Page 15
Film Buff
Order of definitions:
romance, historical, horror, action, science fiction, thriller, western, comedy, war.
Videos:
Romeo & Juliet – Lucy
Psycho – Jane
Saving Private Ryan – Bryn
Star Wars – Calvin

Page 16
Our Free Time
1 He's going to go fishing.
2 She's going to go riding.
3 She's going to go dancing.
4 She's going to go roller skating.
5 He's going to do some photography.
6 He's going to do some painting.
7 He's going to go diving.
8 They're going to go jogging.
9 He's going to go fishing.
10 He's going to go swimming.
11 He's going to go bird watching.
12 She's going to play tennis.
13 She's going to play the guitar.
14 She's going to play chess.

Page 17
On the Road

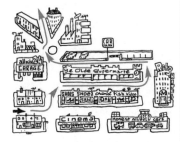

1a 2b 3b 4a 5b 6a 7a
8b

Page 18
In Town
a6 b7 c4 d10 e8 f5 g11
h3 i1 j2 k9
Maggie has been to the library, post office, car park, chemist's, newsagent's and clothes shop.

Page 19
Printer's Mix-up
S & J's Sandwich Bar – 8
Lorna's Ladies' Fashions – 10
Hammer Hardware Store – 11
Mr Watt's Electrical Market – 9
Get Set Hairdresser's – 4
High Street Chemist's – 5
High Heels – 6
Newsagent's – 7   Pork Chop – 1
Rising Dough Baker's – 2
Corner Greengrocer's – 3

Page 20
Going Shopping
Bread rolls – baker's   butter, rice, mushroom soup – grocer's   lettuce, pears – greengrocer's   ham – butcher's   toothpaste – chemist's   lottery ticket – newsagent's

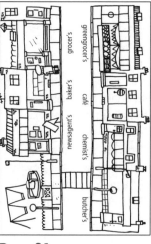

Page 21
Summer Job

Dairy products:	cheese, milk, yoghurt
Frozen foods:	frozen peas, ice cream
Delicatessen:	ham, salami, fresh olives
Poultry:	chicken
Fresh meat:	sausages, chops
Groceries:	pasta, rice, olive oil, ketchup
Beverages:	coffee, tea
Tinned food:	tinned tomatoes
Condiments:	salt, pepper
Cleaning products:	washing-up liquid
Baby products:	nappies
Toiletries:	toothpaste, shampoo
Soft drinks:	Coca Cola
Fresh fruit & vegetables:	apples, bananas, potatoes
Ready-made meals:	Chinese meal or two, lasagne

Page 22
Household Gadgets
1 radio alarm clock   2 mobile phone   3 electric toothbrush
4 hairdryer   5 television & video
6 telephone & fax machine
7 computer & printer   8 toaster
9 microwave   10 dishwasher
11 washing machine
12 fridge-freezer

Page 23
In the Garden
1 apple tree   2 swing   3 pond
4 barbeque   5 path
6 greenhouse   7 wheelbarrow
8 lawnmower   9 vegetable patch   10 statue   11 flower-bed
12 bird-table   13 fountain
14 weeds

Page 24
In the Right Place
1) 1k 2e 3c 4o 5i 6l 7f
8d 9b 10h 11m 12n 13j
14a 15g

2) 2, 5, 6, and 9 are wrong –
2 tub 5 bag 6 can 9 bottle

Page 25
Super Chef!
1) **Menu:** mushroom soup, roast pork, jacket potatoes, fried onions, grilled tomatoes, cheese and biscuits, coffee

2) John's picture is picture C.

3) a frying b boiling
c roasting d grilling e baking

Page 26
You Are What You Eat
Mr Healthy: cereal, fruit juice, yoghurt, an apple, tuna salad, a roll, fruit salad, mineral water, mushroom soup, grilled chicken, peas and potatoes, a banana, furit juice, cereal bar, grapes

Mr Unhealthy: fried eggs, bacon, sausages, beans, coffee with sugar, toast, fish & chips, chocolate mousse, vanilla milkshake, spicy lamb curry, rice & bread, apple pie and cream, tea with sugar, crisps, sweets, chocolate

Page 27
A Family Get-Together
 Denise, Aunt
 Hannah
 Andy, Uncle
 Reg, brother
 Laura, mother
 Julie, sister
 Jim, Father
 Tom, brother-in-law
 Rosa, Cousin
 Olivia
 Fraser

Page 28
Relationships
1 The twins are always playing and chatting. 2 I hate him.
3 At work. 4 Your best friend.
5 Yes, they are friends.
6 The wicked stepmother married Cinderella's father. 7 37
8 She watches his films over and over again. 9 An only child.

10 We have separated.
11 Different. 12 Julian

Page 29
Best Friends
Wendy is Ringo's best friend.
Paula is George's best friend.
Alison is Sue's best friend.
Lorna is John's best friend.

Page 31
How Are You Today?
1) 1 She's freezing.
2 He's thirsty. 3 He's starving.
4 She's ill. 5 He's exhausted.
6 She's scared. 7 He's boiling.
2) I could eat a horse. –
picture 3
I'm feeling under the weather. –
picture 4
I nearly jumped out of my skin. –
picture 6
It's like an igloo in here. –
picture 1.

Page 32
Criminals
1) 1 burglar 2 vandal
3 arsonist 4 pickpocket
5 kidnapper 6 shoplifter
7 thief 8 bank robber
9 smuggler 10 joyrider
2) 1 burglar; video 2 vandal; window 3 pickpocket; phone
4 arsonist; school 5 kidnapper; dog 6 shoplifter; supermarket
7 thief; CD 8 bank robber; money 9 smuggler; suitcase
10 joyrider; cars

Page 33
Crimebusters
1 in court 2 through a window
3 jewellery 4 finger prints
5 sleeping 6 counting a big pile of money 7 no 8 ten o'clock
9 a mask
The suspect is *Chris Cook*.

Page 34
Where Do They Live?
1e 2h 3b 4a 5g 6f
7c 8d

10 Downing Street – The Prime Minister of the UK
The White House – The President of the USA
Buckingham Palace – The Queen of the UK
The Vatican – The Pope

Page 35
What Awful Weather!
1 hailstones 2 storm 3 mist
4 thunder 5 rainbow 6 warm
7 mild 8 drought 9 thaw
10 wind 11 dull 12 lightning
13 grey

Page 36
It's a Sunny Day
1 hot 2 bright 3 scorching
4 sunny 5 suncream
6 sunbathing 7 drought
8 sunglasses 9 heatwave
10 sunburn 11 boiling 12 sun

Page 37
In the Countryside
a field b hedge c tree d stream e hill f path g mud
h birds I nest j leaves k animals l insects m frog
1 hedgehog 2 berries 3 acorn
4 snail 5 pond 6 bee 7 mole

Page 38
This is My Life
1) 1b 2d 3a 4g 5h 6f
7c 8e
2) 2, 3, 4, 8, 7, 1, 6, 5

Page 39
Where Do They Work?
1 hospital 2 school
3 laboratory 4 restaurant

5 studio   6 stables   7 church
8 garage   9 plane   10 office

Page 40
What's My Line?
1 dentist   2 teacher   3 pilot
4 optician   5 footballer   6 civil
servant   7 nurse   8 engineer
9 artist   10 retired   11 secretary
12 student   13 politician
14 doctor   15 butcher
16 waiter   17 housewife
18 shop assistant: this person
works in a shop   19 chef: this
person does the cooking in a
restaurant

Page 41
The Wedding Photo
The clocks on the church show a
different time.
The bride in Picture A has a big
bouquet; the bride in B has a
small one.
In picture B all the men are
wearing carnations in their coats.
In picture A:
– the bridegroom is not wearing
a hat.
– there are flowers on the
bonnet of the car.
– there are two bridesmaids
– the page boys are smiling
– the vicar is talking to a woman
– a woman is taking a photo
– the bridegroom is talking to
the bride

Page 42
Do You Get It?
1 up   2 away   3 home
4 school   5 cold   6 letter
7 angry   8 married   9 lost
10 wet
1-4   2-5   3-7   4-6

Page 43
Doing and Making
1) do: my best, homework, the
shopping, an exam, the
housework
make: a mess, a cake, my bed,
a mistake, a cup of tea, a noise,
an effort

2) 1 Mick made his bed.
2 Mick made a noise.
3 Dick did the shopping.
4 Dick did the housework.
5 Mick made a cake.

Page 44
Idioms
1) A-9-9 B-6-7 C-2-5 D-7-6
E-10-2 F-5-1 G-1-3 H-4-4
I-8-8 J-3-10
3) 1 Hew was angry.
2 He thinks he is wonderful.
3 She is a talented gardener.

Page 45
Early Bird or Night Owl?
1 an alarm clock   2 to snore
3 to selep-walk   4 a dream
5 a lie-in   6 a nightmare
7 to yawn   8 a nap
9 insomniac   10 pyjamas
11 a dressing gown

Page 46
What My Body Does
1 sweat   2 blink   3 sneeze
 4 yawn   5 wink   6 hiccough
7 blush   8 shiver   9 breathe

Page 47
At the Doctor's
1) 1 Leslie   2 Mary   3 Nick
4 Sanjay   5 Alison   6 Jill
7 Seamus   8 Lucy
2) 1 headache – the others are
for putting on wounds
2 accident – the others are
injuries to the skin
3 stomach ache – the rest are
cold symptoms
4 ambulance – the rest are
related to teeth
5 fit – the rest are connected
with sleep

Super Chef

1. John has invited his friends for a special surprise dinner. To know what they are going to eat and drink they need to use the code below. Can you help them?

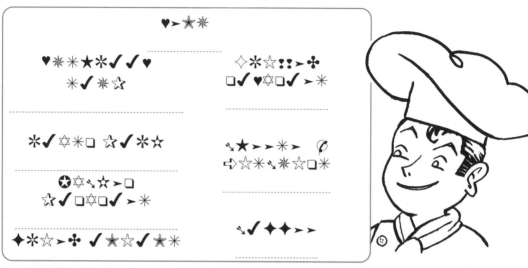

Code

A	B	C	D	E	F	G	H	I	J	K	L	M	N	O	P	Q	R	S	T	U	V	W	X	Y	Z	&

2. Look at the three sets of ingredients. Which are the correct ones for John's meal?

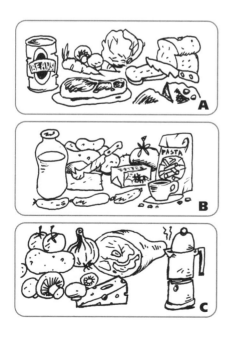

3. John uses different ways to cook his food. Match the pictures below with the ways of cooking. Which methods does John use?

baking

grilling

boiling

frying

roasting

a) ....

b) ....

c) ....

d) ....

e) ....

25

You Are What You Eat

You know that eating too much chocolate and too many chips can be bad for you; however, lots of fresh fruit and vegetables are good for your health. Look at Mr Healthy and Mr Unhealthy. They've both written down all they have eaten today, but unfortunately all the vowels are missing in their lists. Fill the gaps with A E I O U. The pictures will help you.

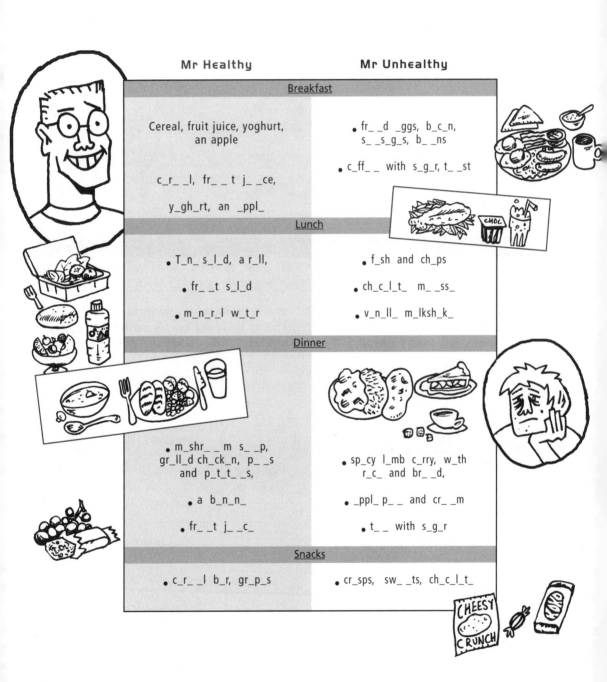

	Mr Healthy	Mr Unhealthy
Breakfast	Cereal, fruit juice, yoghurt, an apple c_r_ _l, fr_ _ t j_ _ce, y_gh_rt, an _ppl_	• fr_ _d _ggs, b_c_n, s_ _s_g_s, b_ _ns • c_ff_ _ with s_g_r, t_ _st
Lunch	• T_n_ s_l_d, a r_ll, • fr_ _t s_l_d • m_n_r_l w_t_r	• f_sh and ch_ps • ch_c_l_t_ m_ _ss_ • v_n_ll_ m_lksh_k_
Dinner	• m_shr_ _m s_ _p, gr_ll_d ch_ck_n, p_ _s and p_t_t_ _s, • a b_n_n_ • fr_ _t j_ _c_	• sp_cy l_mb c_rry, w_th r_c_ and br_ _d, • _ppl_ p_ _ and cr_ _m • t_ _ with s_g_r
Snacks	• c_r_ _l b_r, gr_p_s	• cr_sps, sw_ _ts, ch_c_l_t_

A Family Get-Together

Every Christmas the Tarrant family has a big party. Here they are introducing themselves to John, Sue's fiancé. Can you work out how everyone is related to each other and complete their family tree?

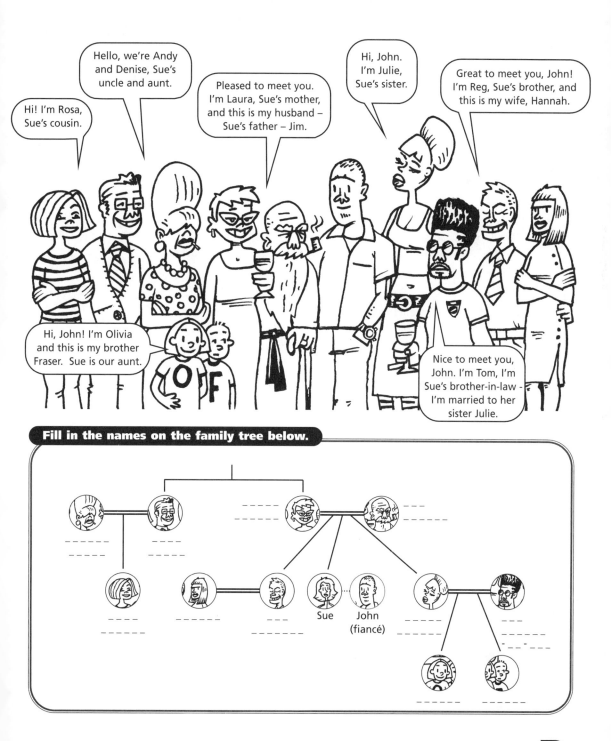

Fill in the names on the family tree below.

Relationships

**Answer the questions in this quiz about people and their relationships.
You will find clues in the pictures.**

1 The twins get on well with each other. Does this mean that they are always fighting and quarrelling or always playing and chatting happily together?

....

2 If I loathe my neighbour. Do I love him or hate him?

....

3 Where do I see my colleagues?

....

4 Who is closer to you? Your best friend or an acquaintance?

....

5 Henry and Sue had a big row, then a few days later they made it up. Are they friends again now or not?

....

6 In the fairytale *Cinderella* the wicked step-mother doesn't want Cinderella to go to the ball. How are Cinderella and the wicked step-mother related?

....

7 Jane is my flatmate and she is also a good friend. I live at 37 Finchley Road. Is Jane's address 37 or 39 Finchley Road?

....

8 My sister idolises Leonardo Di Caprio. Does this mean that she refuses to watch any film with him in it or does she watch all his films over and over again?

....

9 I haven't got any brothers or sisters. Am I an only child or an alone child?

....

10 I have broken up with my fiancé. Does this mean we are getting married soon or we have separated?

....

11 My two children are like 'chalk and cheese'. Are they similar or different?

....

12 Julian is 12, Lucy is 9 and Gary is 6 years old. Who is the eldest in the family?

....

Best Friends

1. Look at the teenagers below. Which pairs are best friends? Use the descriptions to help you.

Sue

George

Paula

Wendy

● The girl who has just got up is still wearing her dressing gown and slippers. Her best friend is the boy wearing a very smart suit.

● The boy wearing trainers, jeans and a stripey T-shirt is best friends with the girl who wears glasses.

● This girl has decided to wear a stripey shirt today.

● The girl wearing flared jeans, glasses and a denim waistcoat is best friends with the boy wearing a bow-tie and leather trousers.

● The girl with the pretty flowery dress and sunhat is best friends with the girl wearing a stripey skirt and colourful ribbons in her hair.

Ringo

Lorna

Alison

John

2. Complete:

Wendy is _____'s best friend.

Paula is _____'s best friend.

Alison is _____'s best friend.

Lorna is _____'s best friend.

Designer Monster

Read the description of the monster. As you read, choose from the pictures on the page and draw your monster in the centre.

scales

claws

hairy ears

pointed ears

square eyes

round eyes

short fur

long nose

curly fur

snout

spikes

black teeth

lumps

antennae

spots

big mouth

small mouth

pointed teeth

- This monster is very big with lots of different textures on his body.
- His arms are covered with short fur, but his legs have scales on them like a fish. He has long black claws on the ends of his fingers and short claws on his toes.
- His stomach is covered with curly fur.
- He has small spikes on his shoulders and small spikes on the top of his head.
- He has three big square eyes and a long nose with spots on it.
- He has a small mouth with black teeth.
- He has lumps on his chin and neck.

How Are You Today?

1. None of the people below are feeling very happy. Use the sentences below to say how they are feeling.

5	He's	exhausted.
☐		starving.
☐		scared.
☐		boiling.
☐		ill.
☐		freezing.
☐		thirsty.

2. Look at the expressions below. Which pictures do they correspond to?

I could eat a horse! Picture _____

I nearly jumped out of my skin! Picture _____

I'm feeling under the weather. Picture _____

Brrrr. It's like an igloo in here. Picture _____

Criminals

1. What types of criminals can you see in these pictures? Use the words in the box and write the name of each type of criminal under the picture.

bank robber	thief	pickpocket	burglar	arsonist
shoplifter	smuggler	joyrider	kidnapper	vandal

2. Now study the pictures again and write the name of the type of criminal in these sentences.

1. The _____ stole a TV and a _____ from the house.

2. The _____ broke the _____ of the phone box.

3. The _____ stole the woman's _____ from her pocket.

4. The _____ set fire to the _____ building.

5. The _____ held the _____ hostage until he got the money he wanted.

6. The manager caught the _____ taking some tins of food from the _____.

7. Joe is a _____. He took a _____ from his friend's room while he wasn't looking.

8. The _____ held up the bank and took a huge amount of _____.

9. The _____ was stopped at Customs. He had a large diamond hidden in his _____.

10. Steve is a _____. He steals people's _____ and drives them around dangerously.

Crimebusters

The Johnson family were burgled last week while they were on holiday. There are three burglars who are well known to the police and one of them was finally arrested yesterday after a complete investigation.

The notorious burglars are:

Chris Cook

Frank Fort

 Marty Sage

---

1. Answer the questions to find out details of the burglary and who the police have arrested. You will find the answers in the picture story.

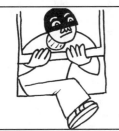  

1. Where is the suspect now? _ _ ◯_ _ _ _

2. How did the burglar break into the house? _ _ _ _ _ _◯ a window.

3. What was stolen? _ _ _ _ _ _ _◯_

4. What did the police find to help them identify the burglar? _◯_ _ _ _ _ _ _ _ _

5. What did the suspect say he was doing when the burglary took place? ◯_ _ _ _ _ _ _

6. What was the suspect doing when he was arrested? ◯_ _ _ _ _ _ _ a big pile of money.

7. Does the suspect have a good alibi? _ ◯, he doesn't.

8. What time did the burglary take place? _ _ _ _'_ _◯_

9. What was the burglar wearing on his face? A _ _ _◯

2. To find the burglar's identity, take the circled letters and his name will be revealed.

⟨ ⟩

Where Do They Live?

Read what the people are saying and then write where each person lives.

a. flat	b. bungalow	c. terraced house	d. detached house
	e. cottage	f. villa	g. mansion	h. bedsit

1. My home is very small and cosy. There are beautiful roses growing around the door.

2. My home is just one room! I cook, eat, sleep and study all in the same room.

3. Our house doesn't have an upstairs, but we have plenty of room and a nice little garden.

4. I haven't got an upstairs or a downstairs! I have a pleasant view from my balcony where I can watch the world go by.

5. My family has lived here for generations. My home has so many rooms that sometimes my guests get lost!

6. I am lucky to have a holiday home in the sun, I spend two months a year here, just relaxing.

7. Our house is quite small and sometimes the neighbours make a lot of noise.

8. We have four bedrooms and a garden because children need plenty of space to play. Luckily we haven't got any neighbours so the children can make as much noise as they want!

Famous addresses!

Do you know who lives in

10 Downing Street?_____

The White House? _____

Buckingham Palace? _____

The Vatican? _____

What Awful Weather!

**Use the clues to help you put the words in the right places in the puzzle.
Each word begins with last letter of the word before it.**

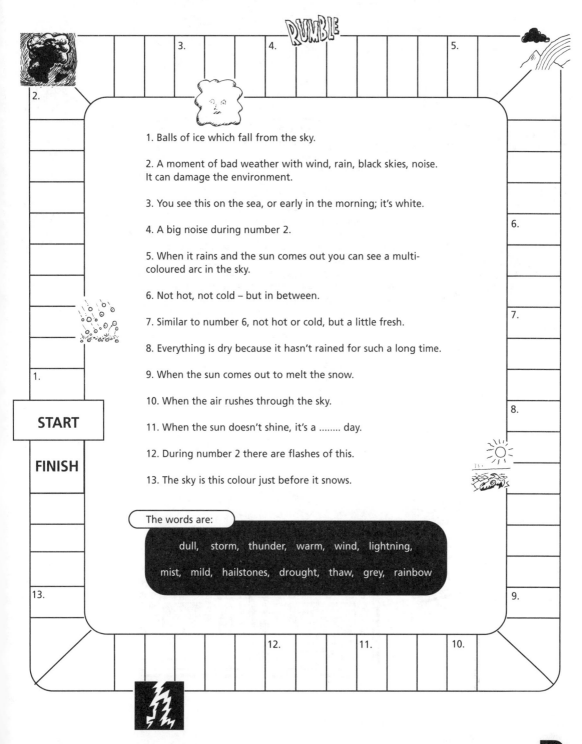

1. Balls of ice which fall from the sky.

2. A moment of bad weather with wind, rain, black skies, noise. It can damage the environment.

3. You see this on the sea, or early in the morning; it's white.

4. A big noise during number 2.

5. When it rains and the sun comes out you can see a multi-coloured arc in the sky.

6. Not hot, not cold – but in between.

7. Similar to number 6, not hot or cold, but a little fresh.

8. Everything is dry because it hasn't rained for such a long time.

9. When the sun comes out to melt the snow.

10. When the air rushes through the sky.

11. When the sun doesn't shine, it's a .... day.

12. During number 2 there are flashes of this.

13. The sky is this colour just before it snows.

The words are:

dull,   storm,   thunder,   warm,   wind,   lightning,

mist,   mild,   hailstones,   drought,   thaw,   grey,   rainbow

START

FINISH

It's a Sunny Day!

Summer is here, the sun is shining and the holiday season has arrived. Complete the puzzle using the clues. All the answers have something to do with the sun.

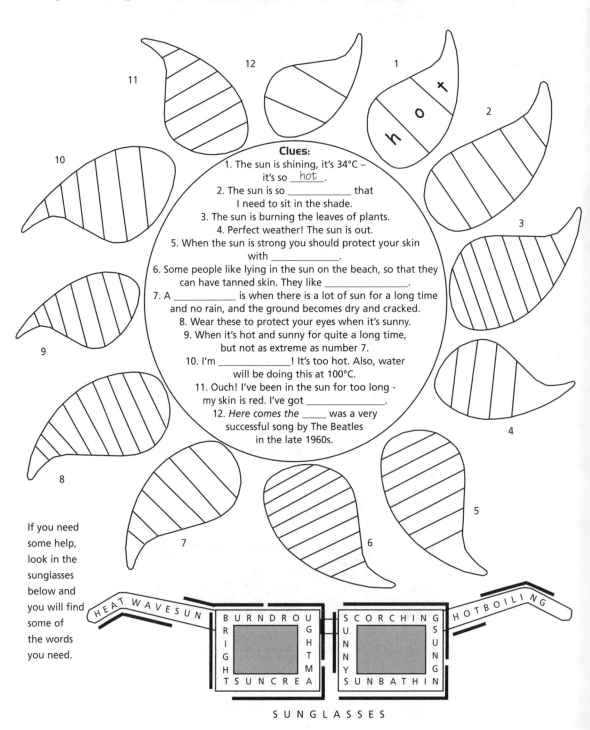

Clues:

1. The sun is shining, it's 34°C – it's so _hot_.
2. The sun is so _____ that I need to sit in the shade.
3. The sun is burning the leaves of plants.
4. Perfect weather! The sun is out.
5. When the sun is strong you should protect your skin with _____.
6. Some people like lying in the sun on the beach, so that they can have tanned skin. They like _____.
7. A _____ is when there is a lot of sun for a long time and no rain, and the ground becomes dry and cracked.
8. Wear these to protect your eyes when it's sunny.
9. When it's hot and sunny for quite a long time, but not as extreme as number 7.
10. I'm _____! It's too hot. Also, water will be doing this at 100°C.
11. Ouch! I've been in the sun for too long - my skin is red. I've got _____.
12. *Here comes the* _____ was a very successful song by The Beatles in the late 1960s.

If you need some help, look in the sunglasses below and you will find some of the words you need.

HEAT WAVE SUN

HOT BOILING

```
B U R N D R O U        S C O R C H I N G
R              G        U              S
I              H        N              U
G              T        N              N
H              M        Y              G
T S U N C R E A        S U N B A T H I N
```

SUNGLASSES

In the Countryside

1. Complete the puzzle. Look at the picture clues and write the words in the correct places.

a.

b.

c.

d.

e.

f.

g.

h.

i.

j.

k.

l.

m.

	1	2	3	4	5	6	7
a.							
b.							
c.							
d.							
e.							
f.							
g.							
h.							
i.							
j.							
k.							
l.							
m.							

2. Now look at these pictures of things you might see on a walk in the countryside. What are they? Use the puzzle to help you work out the words.

For example:

<u>2c 2f 1h 1h 1l 4i</u> = rabbit
r   a   b   b   i   t

 1. 1b 2i 3g 4m 5b 1b 3m 4m

2. 1h 3a 3d 3h 2a 3a 1d

 3. 5k 5l 3m 2c 2l

4. 3i 2k 2f 3k 4e

5. 1f 3m 1i 4h

6. 1h 4l 3c

7. 1g 3m 1j 5b

This is My Life

1. **Match the photos and their descriptions**
2. **Put them in the correct order.**

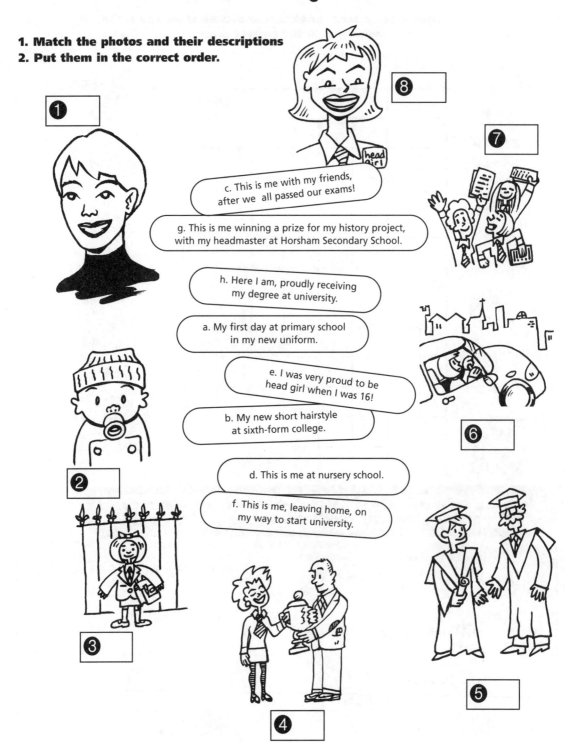

c. This is me with my friends, after we all passed our exams!

g. This is me winning a prize for my history project, with my headmaster at Horsham Secondary School.

h. Here I am, proudly receiving my degree at university.

a. My first day at primary school in my new uniform.

e. I was very proud to be head girl when I was 16!

b. My new short hairstyle at sixth-form college.

d. This is me at nursery school.

f. This is me, leaving home, on my way to start university.

Where Do They Work?

A vet can work in his surgery, on a farm, in a zoo or even in a circus! Find out where you might find other people working. The places are hidden in the boxes.

For example:

Today the policeman is working in the <u>street.</u>

```
w  x  t  t
o  s  d  e
q  r  t  e
```

1. The nurse is working in the _____.

```
x  o  s  e
h  e  p  s
x  d  i  t
s  q  l  a
```

2. Today the headteacher's very busy at _____.

```
p  o  l  k
k  j  l  b
s  x  o  z
c  h  o  d
```

3. The scientist is doing some experiments in the _____.

```
o  y  u  r
y  l  a  o
r  o  b  o
b  t  a  r
```

4. The waiter is serving customers in the _____ .

```
t  y  r  e
n  h  j  s
a  r  t  c
v  u  a  f
```

5. The artist is painting in her _____.

```
e  r  t  u
d  s  t  v
w  x  u  o
v  n  d  i
```

6. The groom is feeding the horses in the _____.

```
s  f  b  r
t  a  f  h
q  d  b  l
c  s  e  n
```

7. The vicar is conducting a wedding in the _____.

```
c  j  i  l
h  j  k  p
v  u  f  h
d  r  c  g
```

8. The mechanic is repairing a car in the _____.

```
l  g  h  o
j  a  r  b
e  f  a  i
x  g  w  z
```

9. The flight attendant is serving coffee on the _____.

```
y  h  u  p
f  g  e  l
j  n  a  g
e  g  b  n
```

10. The accountant is calculating the wages in his _____.

```
p  o  j  k
y  f  h  l
b  m  f  t
e  c  i  b
```

What's My Line?

1. Complete the puzzle, using the clues to help you. All the answers are jobs and professions. When you've finished, you should have the answers to numbers 18 and 19. Can you write the definitions of these two jobs?

Clues

This person ...

1. helps you when you have toothache.
2. works in a school and gives you homework.
3. flies a plane.
4. tests your eyes and fits your glasses.
5. is a well-paid sportsman.
6. works for the state, in government and public offices.
7. looks after patients in a hospital.
8. designs machines, roads, bridges.
9. is a painter, musician, actor, sculptor.
10. doesn't work anymore. (This person has finished his/her working life.)
11. is an essential assistant to the boss, takes the boss's calls and deals with correspondence.
12. hasn't started working yet, and is at university or college.
13. is elected to represent a town, and could be a minister in parliament.
14. examines you when you are ill.
15. prepares and sells meat.
16. serves food in a restaurant.
17. stays at home and looks after her children.

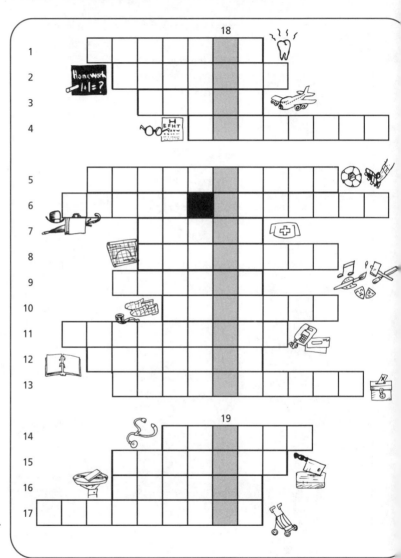

Number 18: This person

....

....

....

....

Number 19: This person

....

....

....

....

The Wedding Photo

There are ten differences between picture A and B. Write sentences, for example:
"The bridegroom isn't wearing a hat in B but he is in A."
The words in the box will help you.

bride   bridegroom   bridesmaid   best man   page-boy   vicar   bouquet   church   wedding guests
confetti   wedding car

Do You Get It?

**Hidden in the grid below are expressions used with the verb to get.
Look at the first line. The answer is: *get up*.
Can you find the other hidden words and match them with the correct pictures? There
is one word hidden in each line of the grid.**

1 f e t y x x (u p) r z z
2 h t a w a y k v b c e
3 h o m e r g j y s e c
4 b e m o s c h o o l a
5 t y u f c o l d o o h
6 p l e t t e r d h j u
7 l m u a n g r y d e z
8 p o i m a r r i e d p
9 p o l u l o s t h t u
10 b n w e t y h y g d g

1 get ....up..............

2 get ....

3 get ....

4 get to ....

5 get a ....

6 get a ....

7 get ....

8 get ....

9 get ....

10 get ....

**Do you know which of the
above expressions with get
can be replaced with the
following?**

1 to arrive at – number ....

2 to catch – number ....

3 to become – number ....

4 to receive – number ....

Doing and Making

1. Dick is a snail who does things and Mick is a snail who makes things. Read round their shells to find the expressions with do and make.

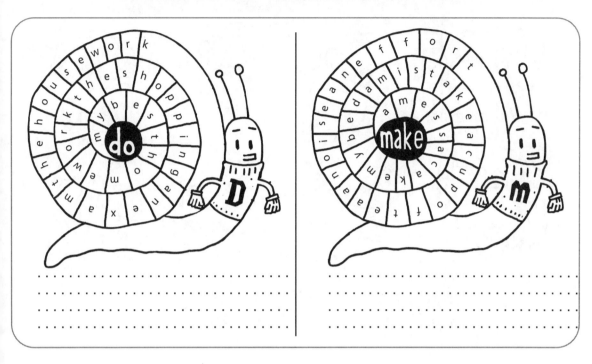

. . . .
. . . .
. . . .
. . . .

2. Look at the cartoons. Identify the snail and say what each one did yesterday.

Idioms

1. Look at the cartoons. They all represent a common idiom in English. Match the correct idiom with each cartoon. Then match each idiom with its correct meaning.

Idioms
1. My exam was <u>a piece of cake</u>!
2. It's really <u>not my cup of tea</u>.
3. I <u>slept like a log</u>.
4. <u>I could eat a horse</u>.
5. I felt <u>like a fish out of water</u>.
6. He's always <u>got ants in his pants</u>!
7. He <u>drinks like a fish</u>.
8. I can <u>smell a rat</u>.
9. He is the <u>black sheep</u> of the family.
10. Robert is <u>the teacher's pet</u>.

Meanings
1. To feel out of place.
2. The teacher's favourite pupil.
3. Something is very easy.
4. To be really hungry.
5. To dislike something.
6. To drink too much alcohol.
7. A person who can't sit still for long.
8. To suspect something suspicious about a situation or a person.
9. Someone who is always in trouble and brings shame to his family.
10. To sleep really well.

2. Are any of these idioms the same in your language?

3. What do you think the following idioms mean?

1. Jules was like a bear with a sore head this evening. I wonder what upset him at work?
2. He thinks he is the bee's knees. But actually he isn't any better than anyone else!
3. Her garden looks beautiful. She must have green fingers.

Early Bird or Night Owl?

All the words are related to bedtime and sleeping. Find the missing consonants in each picture to complete them.

1.

k
c
l
r

c
l
m
n

a _   a _ a _ _ _ o _ _

11.

s
n
d
n
w

s
g
r
g

a _ _ e _ _ i _ _ - _ o _ _

10.

y
j
s

p
m

_ _ _ a _ a _

9.

m

n   n   c
s

i _ _ o _ i a _

2.

t n r s

ZZZ!

_ o _ _ o _ e

8.

ZZZz

p
n

a _ a _

3.

zzzzZ

s
t
k
w

p
l
l

_ o _ _ _ ee _ _ a _ _

5.

ZZ
n
l

a _ i e - i _

7.

n
w

y
t

_ o _ a _ _

4.

d   r

m

a _ _ e a _

6.

h

m
n
g
r

a _ i _ _ _ a e

What My Body Does

The pictures show things our bodies do. Match the verbs and the pictures.

| shiver | blush | blink | sweat | yawn | wink | sneeze | hiccough |

1. _ _ _ _

2. _ _ _ _ _

3. _ _ _ _ _ _

4. _ _ _ _

5. _ _ _ _

6. _ _ _ _ _

7. _ _ _ _ _

8. _ _ _ _ _

9. What do our bodies do all the time, even when we are asleep? Rearrange the circled letters above and find the verb.

_ _ _ _ _ _ _

At the Doctor's

1. Look at the people in the doctor's waiting room. Read their comments below and write their names under their pictures.

2. Look at the following lists of words. Circle the odd one out in each list. Say why it is the odd one out.

For example:

nurse   surgeon   (patient)   doctor   dentist

Patient is the odd one out because the others are people who look after and treat patients.

1.   plaster ointment bandage headache antiseptic cream

2.   cut scratch wound accident   3.   cough sneeze stomach-ache sore throat runny nose

4.   X-ray dentist filling toothache ambulance   5.   tired fit sleepy exhausted

Material written by: **Julie Woodward**

Project Editor: **Judith Greet**

Designers: **Tracey Mason**, **Victoria Wren**, **Caroline Grimshaw**

Cover design: **Kaya-anne Cully**

Illustrations by: **Chris Watson**

Mary Glasgow Magazines, an imprint of Scholastic Inc., 2003

Printed in the UK by Ashford Colour Press Ltd, Gosport, Hampshire